i can't let the thoughts go

they collect

mountains out of molehills

oceans out of streams

tears out of my eyes

all because of you

the thoughts of you in my

very
     very

        very
                 *scattered mind*

*index*

dear reader,

if these words come to you at a time in your life you so
desperately want to end- let them give you hope. let them lift
you up and give you the wings you needed to fly out of the
damned hell hole called your mind- that tends to overthink
everything.
i hope each phrase brings sunshine and clarity to the dark cloud
that hangs over your head.
and lastly, i hope you see how special you are
that someone loves you
and that you're not alone

- naveen rimah

heart

blooming garden love

reaching into the depths of

the unknown i seek

## who was i before you broke my heart?

who was i before you broke my heart?

a lonely girl, wandering the streets of self-worth

hooked on the idea that love was a thing

before you broke my heart i was intrigued by you

i ignored my constant anxiety and fear that this- you were all a
lie
my conscience wasn't

weighed down by dark clouds of depression
i wasn't slowly chipping away

before you broke my heart i was vulnerable, ready to open
myself to someone who would

understand

who would

love

that person was not you

i will never go back to the girl i was before you broke my heart
and maybe

that's a good thing

you lit a fire and left

it seems that you have

no regrets

and i

regret nothing

except the beginning of it all

*beginning of it all*

*i wonder*

sometimes i wonder if you even remember me

remember the way we used to talk

those words dripped with potential hope for a future
with us in it

a future that didn't come true

did it mean the same to you?

now when i think of your name i just feel blue

it's funny to think there would even be a me & you

a hopeless romantic meets a broken boy at the
most unexpected time

and i'm just that

over feeling

over loving

only to get hurt in the end

*no one compares*

no one compares;

to your sweet love

lifting me up, up above

where the world is brand new- with the addition of you

told me you cared

*the hook*

heart and soul wrung until dry

throat horse

i play your lies

words

echoing throughout my complex mind

again

   and again

      the hook keeps on going

*what is love?*

is it the endless cycle of moments you go over
with them in your head?

is it the fluttery feeling in your chest
when you see

them. the person you would risk anything for. no matter how
many times they hurt you

is it the pain: the feeling of your heart squeezing
itself when you can't see them soon. or ever again?

is it the happiness

erupts inside your lungs. taking your breath away making you
see stars

you would do anything to see them smile

is it the fact

that even though some moments are so hard

something about them. the way they hold you. the way they say
your name. makes you hold on and stick it out?

is it the fact that us: humans can never be the same without it

is it the you would never be the same without it?

## will i ever

will i ever let go of my false memory of you?

will i ever leave the sad memories behind,

moving on to make new

will i ever, lift my head up high and
not constantly be afraid to cry

over you

who broke me

who shook me, until i couldn't stand

will i even get over the sad emptiness of a feeling
that haunts me in the night

will i ever?

maybe i won't

or maybe...

i will

starry sky

whispered night

love at heart

i come alive

*come alive*

i wear my heart on my sleeve like an accessory

throwing out last seasons- it gets the best of me

i give, the world around me

lives

without me

fine

*heart*

*when he was with her*

running over the thoughts that

jumble her chaotic mind

throwing them out

deemed useless

she then grew

thick skin

that is, but why?

did she still stay with him?

*the colors in your eyes*

lighting up the deepest night

when you smile

i find myself captivated

by

the bottomless pits

of your dark brown eyes

that seem to hold the secrets

of the world

out of those lips

your words conduct symphony's

*his magic*

when he said those simple words

instead of a smartass remark i shut up

and let my heart do the talking

*i knew i loved him*

my heart will burst from the overwhelming

weight of my love

when i see you again

my heart will crack from the

overwhelming

thought of not seeing you soon

when i say goodbye

*hardest goodbye*

*seasons*
your love came in seasons. the rough or gentle
transitions of thoughts, feelings- always
including my small dose of self-doubt.

the blossoming of newfound love started
in spring- nothing seemed rushed. perfect bliss

that went all too fast before the hot gazes of others scorched
our unprotected skin. then you adapted to the sun

and changed yourself- i refused to, change myself for others.
as the whispy leaves fell from the color changing trees,
it seemed like you never needed me.

you switched up as fast as fall became winter.
as splinters of my heart fell like snowflakes
in the harsh winter breeze- i thought maybe
i knew you.

turns out i never did.

her honey bob bounced

when she walked

sang- when she spoke

like every word was sung on a key

her lips parted with intention

her mind an invention

a renaissance girl

_serenity_

it's funny that your father

taught you how to walk on the outside of the sidewalk

but didn't teach you how to not break a girl's heart

*life lessons*

i wonder what it'd be like

to be adored like the sun

rising- a breathtaking entrance

that baffles and blesses the

eyes or mortals

*true beauty*


the sky dips down to

vibrant darkness

as the stars spot across

the canvas-like sky

creating poetry in the still night

the fact that i still worry about you

while i'm lying in bed

is giving you more than i intended to

*daydreams*

sugarcoated memories

and a hazy conscience

"it will be okay" he tells me

"but how" i ask, "when my heart feels empty when you're gone"

*promises*


you tell me that i know damn well you care

well actions speak louder than words

show me you do

maybe than i'll understand

the memories are the things that haunt me. i can see your handsome face and devilish smirk every day. i can see you walk the halls with your chin up, eyes meeting mine. i can deal with knowing you're not with me and maybe with her. but when certain things happen that remind me of the memories- the simple yet breathtaking moments shared together; that's when my heart feels like its shattering into a million pieces.

*memories make the heart die faster*

their "i love you" may seem sincere

but look and lean closer darling

and listen to what their soul says

*reminders I*

*"i want to fix this"*

which part

the pain from the first goodbye

or the heartache from the second

it seems like everything you do i'm all for you. you tell me that i'm beautiful, make me happy when the days feel blue. the hardships, the struggles, the arguments and misinterpreted messages. i want to work it out. through and through. i'll always be right here for you.

you told me that you're done. done with us and now i'm here thinking what have i done. why have i fucked up something beautiful with my mess of emotions. you say i still don't make you unhappy. yet i feel like i've failed.

so i wrote you an apology. a typed-out portion of my heart that currently has no response. pledging my allegiance to you. it tells you all the things i needed to say, how i'm always willing to work it out. how i'm so sorry if i took you for granted. how it feels like i'm empty when i'm without you. that i'm all for you.

i sit waiting for a response. i hope you give us another chance- agree to talk out our misunderstandings. but maybe you wont. maybe you will stand by your word and turn around and never look back.

a piece of my heart will crack when you leave

_all for you_

why do i tell myself that this tainted love is worth it

that you're worth it

body

sensations that flow
through my pulsing body
begging not wanting

*slipping away*

i'm slipping away.

i can feel it.

my body descending into the cool

unforgiving waters of depression

my hair wild-

floating aimlessly around my buzzing brain

and you;

you let go.

my body yearns for the feelings of your hands on my skin in places i have not been touched before

the feeling of your lips against mine

knowing your mind

my thighs clench together in anticipation

i shouldn't give into this fantasy

_dirty thoughts_

i tell myself i will never do that again

yet here i am

_patterns of the heart_

leaves drift as my clothes fall

wind moves through our tangled branches

*autumn*

our magnetic hands quickened

as our static hearts shook

two electric souls met

in the heat of the dark

*electric souls*

the quickened pulse flowing through our veins

drugged us

making us see an alternate reality

one without pain

oh

how we long for that to be true

*alternate reality*

your voice awakens a tide in me

even when you're saying her name

*lip-reading in candlelight*

i see how you tend to

admire the things i do

with a stern face and sharp expressions

i see your eyes watching my careful movements

and i smile




                                        you remind me of a mountain

                                              when you're mad

                                hardening expressions of a man

                                                    *frown*

sticks and stones

broke my bones

pretend that words never hurt me

letting down my wall of doubt

bringing in positivity

*sticks and stones*

darkness trickling through

your honey coated eyes

untold secrets and lies

*untold*

holds herself like an angel

but don't take for granted

what really goes on behind

those oh so innocent eyes

touching is not always

the right way to feel connection

please hold me close first


held me close when he broke my heart

kissed my lips when she lied

enough, enough

i told myself

last time i would cry

_enough, enough_

i want to count the freckles on your face

memorize the patterns in your waves

look into your eyes

and see your view of the world

touch your soul with my body

trace constellations with your hands

until i understand

how you hold all the world


                                        bodies weaving a

                    complex pattern that's called love?

                              seems like it's only lust

when i touched him

i felt his pain

dripping down my fingers

i desperately tried

to make it all better




a skeleton of a

man

and yet

i still stayed

*and yet*

## *fine*

tell me all the little lies

you'd whisper in my ear

the ones that made me feel

near to you- you're so far away

the ones i knew were

fake

believed so my heart

wouldn't break

into a thousand pieces

and you'd move on

fine

you make it so damn easy to fall in love

*devilish smile*

i pick the rose despite the thorn

reaching out- i swore

i'd be careful

it pricks me anyways

*thorn*


                              the window to the soul

                          and lost memories collide

                        in the way, you look at me my

                                            eyes

                            stare back with longing

                          trying to figure you out

it's funny that

when you're making love to that beautiful girl

whose eyes linger on each of your movements

and heart beats just for you

you'll be thinking- imagining me

the way my lips part when i speak

mind works in ways you could never really

understand

how my soul speaks

and yours aches for me

the girl that you once

let go and is now

free

*a mirage of a girl you once knew*

when you see, the stars think of me

how you could make constellations

with the blemishes on my face

connect the stars in my eyes

and craters in my heart

even though you're with her

i still see the way you look at me

like I'm holding something you need

it baffles me how you can let me go, and still act like you want
me




you left me so quickly for

a girl you've been waiting for

yet- she reached out when it was continent for her

sometimes it makes me wonder if you ever even cared

*doubt*

how do you feel when you find out

the girl you gave everything for is boring?

she does not speak her mind

her words do not roll of her tongue like honey

eyes holding secrets

heart beating for you- only

because you are her flavor of the week

and you will stay giving, wanting

forgetting and discarding a woman

who did all the things she never will

when your heart seems to break into

a thousand pieces

of lost love and painful memories

you reminisce about the times

when you kissed

play- and touched

sexual feelings overwhelming

filling the void

and distracting you from the fact

that he was never yours

the smooth curves of a valley

divots of streams

flat surfaces are there but

hard to find perfection

in mother earths imprints on my body

when all i see is

wrecked land from a storm

*earth's imprints*


                                    my body is mine

                    a temple, fortress of womanhood

                         all bundled up i let it undo

                           hair grows, garments off

                                    i expose myself

                                 to the world daily

                          but not enough to myself

                                   *self-love is key*

yearn for something

unspoken yet

spoken through

the whirlwind

of tongue, soul reaching for yours




i don't see you anymore
        only fragments of the person you used to be

*glass heart*

*things that remind me of you*

1. the eternal warmth when i drink a cup of tea

2. cold afternoons

3. sunlight on my bedsheets

4. walking empty hallways

5. dents in lockers

6. peppermint tea

7. the very faint smell of cigarettes mixed with cologne and an indescribable smell that makes me feel at home

8. wrapping my arms around myself

9. the sounds of sneakers

10. the sound of lighters

11. almonds

12. that specific stairwell

13. hallway lights shining into dark classrooms

14. the night

15. watercolor

16. melancholy moments while listening to soft songs

17. every time someone touches my hand

*you say you want me*

all of me?

or the just the parts sexualized?

do you not only want to touch my soft curves but yearn to treat
them with the respect they deserve

not tear apart my body but become one with it

do you fantasize about my complex mind, wanting to know
more

truly- not just the surface of my breast and the side of my hips

thickness of thighs you say you so desperately crave

but flinch at the waves that come crashing down with them

seems you're not ready for a woman like me

make music with my sounds

familiarize your hands with the divots in my hips and marks on
my thighs

tender touches, turning rough- slow- down for a moment and
savor the taste

of my lips on yours

before you consume me

*consume me*

she will never be me

no matter how hard she tries

silly woman- be yourself

for if it is you he truly loves

he won't care in the end

*copycat*

i wish i could go back and watch myself fall for you

so i could see the exact moment i decided to settle for someone
who wasn't worth my time

and call it love

_broken clocks_


i find it frustratingly funny

the fact that you can tell me all the things i want to hear

claim that you obsess over my soft curves and fantasize about
my complex mind

while you pursue her

a girl who will never be me

_your cravings_

i wonder when you hurt her

if she'll feel my pain too

my heart cracking, tears dripping

i don't cry for her

i cry for myself too


do not tell me

what to say and when to say it

as if the words that roll off my tongue is something you should
be able to control

do not tell me

what to wear and when to wear it

as if the clothes i lay on my skin should be easily accessible to
you

because that's all i am

a toy- for you to dispose of on a later date

*my skin*

she might want to believe the best in him is yet to blossom

but she needs to remember that is not her responsibility to tend
to the thorns bound to prick her in the end

*garden of eden*

explore the parts of me

others claimed inhabitable

too scared to journey along the dangerous valley called my
curves

and dive headfirst into my soul

*exploration*

my head knows better

yet the devil in my heart yearns for your touch

*despite it all*

soul

emotions left me

broken and bruised i remember

you never knew my soul

*flowerchild*

plucked from the earth

she was only newly blossomed

they told her to

sing- flowerchild sing

the never-ending song of change

and plant it within us

and it will grow

today

a beaming smile

took me awhile

to keep it this way

broken heart

mended to one

it finally stayed

in the sunlight

i watch myself grow with pride

*grow*

i'm scared of the leap

the moment of sheer flight

where you're in the middle

thinking about the decision you just made

doesn't help because there is

nothing

you can do about it

*i see you*

in the way, the wind moves through the trees. the way you used to hold me.
before you were brittle and weak. before you said the last words, you would speak.

it's not always the past that haunts us, it's the idea of moving forwards. without you- it is to me.

i cannot explain the pain of losing you other than saying it felt like infinity.
the world seeming so far away and incomplete compared to what you are seeing in front of your eyes.
everything.
absolutely everything. the in's, the out's, the up's, the downs. you- i felt it.
it's almost too much to wrap your head around.
but when you do, it feels like the whole world is crashing down on your shoulders.
and no one can lift it up.
that's death.
1-12-12

she sits in her chair

the chaos of drama surrounding her. bustling, rushing, loud

but she is, still. she sits lost in her own thoughts. that are not so

but to handle them she stays still

if she is not she will drown herself in her own sorrow, rip at the binds that keep her tears from flowing.

out

she is still. it settles her wild thoughts and prevents her from overthinking the smallest detail

she is still. like a boulder in a river, people rush past spewing hateful words

there was a time when there was no still-nes settling over her inexpressive face.

*still*

cup half empty

i continue to pour

out- it trickles down into doubting hearts and minds

but leaves me empty

still giving more

*half empty*

*garden*

the roots of my problems start far away

as i try to dig the weeds from my brain

new blossoms

ideas at play

hosing down stress

day

to

day

the overgrown vines seem to have found a home

in the hole in my heart

that i tried to fill with stones

fabricated memories

seem to make me less

lonely

in the early hours of the day

_lonely_




i miss a voice that i barely remember

a touch

only of a photograph handing on my wall

and through it all

I still remember

your

_smile_

it's crazy how i breathe in

and only let it out

when i fall

*breathtaking*

are we lost until someone finds us

or are we lost until we find ourselves
_lost_

when a lively soul

meets a broken one

in the dark night

a spark of realization

comes alive inside

these two souls

alike- yet not the same

realize it's better to be

together than apart

hence, balancing each other out

*yin and yang*

to all the girls

who have been told to swallow their words

and put a smile on their beautiful face

told that speaking out

is unattractive and they should be

ashamed

of their "outrageous" opinion

not be proud of the way their eyes flash with passion

and smile grows when they realize

they can change the world

*the future is female*

*sunflower*

a free spirit on a lonely

night trip

seeking something they've

yet to find

something

amidst the squinting eyes

bright as day

on top of dark night

a sign perhaps a

coincidence of sheer luck

to notice the things worth finding

sometimes you must take a closer look

*how to lose yourself*

first you do things for others. nothing is ever for you anymore

you just wait for them, disregarding any. second thoughts are non-existent

when days blend together and nights seem like mornings.

you go about doing the same thing each day. instead of loving something you
love someone.

giving away your own sense of self for a sense of love- that is only lust.

is what you eat in the morning, work for in the evening, and lie awake thinking about at night.

your own thoughts are dismissed. Instead focusing on a thing that is taking away the "you" in "you and me" waiting for the day

when my thoughts can become one

with my calming soul




with my calming soul

when my thoughts can become one

waiting for the day

that i can express equally

instead of taking from one

giving to another

part of me left empty

needing attention i lack

a scattered mind with a

growing soul

bloom later i say

there is always time for you

to blossom with pride

*bloom later*

rising to the sun

i stay growing today

as i water myself

i wish the never-ending flow of life would just

stop- for a quick moment

just so i could get the hang of things for once

*wishes I*

the only person you can be is yourself. the quicker you accept that
the better your life will be.

don't let the negativity strip away your soul everyday

it gets better

the pain will eventually come to an end and the cycle of disastrous
things will stop. I know this sounds like a stretch but i'm not shitting
you

life does indeed get better

so, lift your chin up and remember who the fuck you are

*a letter to my past self*

## *blackhole*

pull in my collecting doubts

hook on my scattered mind

tell my broken heart mountain

of believable lies

grab- the attention on my wandering eyes

and show it how to focus on the

blackhole

forming inside

## about the author

while writing *scattered mind*, naveen thought about how the world and our experiences affect us as humans, along with the little things in life. the things we can't shake. writing about doubt, love, loss, and lust- naveen strives to help people understand and notice the little things about themselves and the world around them with her poetry.

as well as writing poetry, naveen enjoys music, vinyl records, chilly nights and rainy mornings. she believes that pessimism is not in fact a negative thing and that no one will ever truly know every part of themselves.

instagram:

@naveenrimah

&

@rimahpoetry

Made in the USA
Middletown, DE
10 February 2021

33509344R00046